Living in
VENICE

Robert Moore

Silver Burdett

Series and book editor: Belinda Hollyer
Designer: Sally Boothroyd
Picture researcher: Suzanne Williams
Production controller: John Moulder

Consultant: J. G. Links

The author would like to thank Elena Casimiro and Pierluigi Santini for their help during the preparation of the text.

The editor would also like to record her thanks to Adriano Carrettin, the late owner of the Locanda Montin in Venice.

Cover picture: The Rio San Lorenzo. Early morning shoppers are already out, and the outdoor café tables are set up for business. You can see racks of postcards at the newspaper stall – and one of the first gondola trips of the day.

Endpapers: Looking down the Grand Canal, towards San Marco, from the Rialto Bridge. The Canal is the "main street" of Venice, into which more than 40 smaller canals flow. There are traditional striped mooring poles in front of some of the buildings, but the plain wooden piles are now more common.

Title page: A group of young Venetians pause on a bridge on their way to school.

Contents page: An arched stone window in an old house provides both a handy spot to grow geraniums, and a vantage point from which to view the passing world.

Adapted and published in the
United States in 1986 by
Silver Burdett Company,
Morristown, N.J.

Artists
ESR Ltd: main map and area map 42-43
Julia Osorno: 41
Jenny Sanders: 19, 20-21, 22-23, 42-43

Photographic sources

Key to position of pictures:
(T) top, (C) center, (R) right, (L) left, (B) bottom

Accademia, Venice (photo Bridgeman Art Library): 9B
Biblioteca Nazionale Mariana, Venice: 8
Nick Birch: 25TL
Colorific: 22(S. McCartney), 24TL(P. Boucas), 24CR(M. Yamashita), 34-35B (G. Tortoli), 40B
Daily Telegraph Colour Library/Adam Woolfitt: contents page, 16-17, 28, 30T and 35 (Explorer)
Gernsheim Collection: 18T
Susan Griggs Agency/Adam Woolfitt: 32, 34T
Robert Harding Picture Library: 12-13 (J.G. Ross), 32B
Museo Marciana, Venice (photo SCALA): 9T
NASA: 40-41T
The National Gallery, London: 11B
The Naya Collection/Osvaldo Böhm Archives, Venice: 10, 18B
The Photo Source/CLI: endpapers
The Photographers' Library: 13
The Procuratoria of San Marco, Venice: 11T
Sarah Quill: 30B, 33, 37B, 38, 39T
Rex Features Ltd: 17B, 29B, 36
Spectrum Colour Library: 14-15
Patrick Thurston: 26-27T
ZEFA: 19, 23

All other photographs by Robert Moore

Library of Congress Cataloging in Publication Data

Moore, Robert, 1942–
    Living in Venice.

    (City life) (Silver Burdett library selection)
    Includes index.
    Summary: Text and photographs depict various aspects of life in one of the world's most unusual cities built on the mud banks and islands of the Venetian lagoon. Includes information about its history, famous sites, markets, daily life, festivals and celebrations, and modes of transportation in a city whose principal streets are canals.
    1. Venice (Italy)—Social life and customs—Juvenile literature.   [1. Venice (Italy)—Social life and customs]
I. Title   II. Series.
DG675.6M597   1985   945'.31   85-40305
ISBN 0-382-09116-7

Contents

Rise to power

There was never meant to be a city on the mud banks and islands of the Venetian lagoon. Neither sea nor land, this shallow waste was formed by the silty waters of several big rivers as they flowed into the Adriatic Sea.

But in the early 6th century a number of Christian communities, fleeing from persecution on the mainland, took refuge here. These pioneers had to live by their wits. They trapped fish and wild birds, and sold the only other products of the lagoon – driftwood, and salt, a precious commodity. Soon they were also guiding ships and ferrying goods through the treacherous channels and tides of their primitive and marshy home. In time they began to prosper as traders and merchants. The first brick, and then stone, churches and forts were built, and a single ruler for the scattered communities, the first Doge (duke), was elected.

The beginnings of a city

One particular group of islands, clustered around the *rivo alto* (high bank) of a wide, deep channel, became especially prosperous. When the Doge moved there early in the 9th century, the city of Venice was born. This channel was later called the Grand Canal, and was spanned by its Rialto (*rivo alto*) Bridge.

Venice grew as medieval Europe grew, fully exploiting its position at the crossroads of East-West trade. In the haven of the lagoon, protected from the mainland by marshes and from the open sea by sand bars, Venice built up its muddy islands and developed a fleet of ships. It was probably the first city to live by trade alone.

The Venetian Empire

An enormous shipbuilding yard, the Arsenal, became famous throughout Europe. From here convoys of galleys and sailing ships set forth, laden with raw materials from Europe. They returned with rich cargoes from the East, of spices and luxury goods such as gold, jewels, silks – and slaves. The tall *campanile* (bell-tower) was a beacon for these ships. The city grew in splendor as their cargoes enriched the palaces built by the new class of merchants, bankers and business men. And

Venetian workmen became skilled in such exotic crafts as glassmaking, and working in precious metals and stones.

Venice had secured a virtual monopoly of the spice trade, so fighting ships were needed to defend both the cargo ships and the ever-increasing number of far-flung trading colonies. The colonies stretched down the Adriatic coasts through the Greek islands and beyond, eventually to include Crete and Cyprus in a great maritime Empire. The Adriatic Sea was called the Gulf of Venice.

Enterprise and opportunity

No commercial opportunity was missed. Venice made great profit from the Crusades – the series of wars in which Christian Europe tried to recapture the Holy Land from the Muslims. Above all, the conquest of Constantinople in 1204, during the Fourth Crusade, gave Venice an almost incalculable amount of treasure.

In all this, Venice's secret was, as one writer put it, "never take sides and always have the best ships in Europe." Venice also achieved and maintained power through the form of government evolved by its citizens. Though

Above: This picture, from a 16th century manuscript, shows what the first 6th century settlements in the lagoon may have looked like. The timber-framed houses have walls of dried mud and roofs of thatched reed: all lagoon materials.

Right: Part of a 15th century painting by Carpaccio, showing a religious procession passing over the old Rialto Bridge. In the 900 years separating this picture from the scene above, Venice had grown into the greatest city in Europe. Yet just as the basic character of the city can be seen in the earlier picture, so many of today's details – the chimneys, roof terraces and drying clothes, and many of the same buildings – are recognizable here.

Right: This 14th century painting records part of the story of St. Mark, the patron saint of Venice. In 828, the Venetian rulers decided to replace their original patron saint, Theodore, with the more powerful and important Mark. His body was stolen from Alexandria, in Egypt, and brought to Venice by ship. Here, the sailors are being guided through treacherous rocks by a vision of St. Mark himself. The first church of St. Mark was built to house his bones, and the lion of St. Mark — the symbol of the saint — became the symbol of Venice too.

not a democracy in the modern sense, it was certainly unique in medieval Europe. Under the symbolic leadership of the Doge, Venice was a Republic, ruled by committees of citizens from the leading families. This system was so intricately and shrewdly organized that it lasted for over a thousand years.

The Serene Republic

In the changeless government of *La Serenissima* – the most serene Republic – the greater glory and commercial health of the Republic always came first. Nothing was left to chance. Individual ambition was crushed, and trade secrets, such as the making of mirrors, were ruthlessly protected. At home, stability was guaranteed by a remarkably fair code of justice. Abroad, in order to promote and protect their interests, the Venetians virtually invented international diplomacy, a combination of high-level selling and cloak-and-dagger intrigue. And to sustain their great operations, these intensely practical people developed the most sophisticated banking system in medieval Europe: survivors, pioneers and opportunists first and last.

Decline from glory

The Venetian Republic always had a fleet of warships at sea, either defending or extending trade routes. In the 14th century a momentous decision was taken: the Venetian lion, symbol of the Republic, was to "step ashore" and attack the powerful city-states disrupting its trade on the mainland.

In a series of battles (later recorded on the walls and ceilings of the Great Hall in the Doge's Palace), the armies of Venice overcame those of many other city-states, including Padua, Verona and Milan. Their great rival, Genoa, had already been defeated in an epic battle in the lagoon itself. The Republic, ruler of the seas, now also possessed a great land empire in northern Italy.

A power in decline
Yet just at this time, when Venice was at the very peak of its fame, events occurred which marked its eventual decline. In 1508 some other European countries united in an attempt to crush Venetian power and ambition. The Republic survived seven years of war, but its resources were severely tested. More seriously still, the Venetian commercial empire had been threatened by two earlier events: the taking of Constantinople by the Turks in 1453, and the opening of new trade routes to the East by Vasco da Gama in 1498.

At first barely a tremor was felt through the Republic. Indeed, when the new ideas and arts of the Renaissance reached Venice, the city enjoyed a period of renewed artistic splendor. Many great artists decorated its palaces and churches, further enriching the legendary city with a style of painting uniquely Venetian.

The pressure of change
In many ways the city was more productive and resourceful than ever. Armies of citizens still toiled in the factories turning out glass, mirrors and ships; in hundreds of workshops Venetian craftsmen wrought exquisite items of gold, jewelry and armor. New industries such as wool and silk manufacture had been developed, and Venice now led the world in printing and publishing. But its richest and most powerful citizens were turning from business and government to cultivating their new estates on the *terra firma* (mainland). The great days of the Republic were numbered. Venetian trade was faced with real competition, and Venetian ships and convoys were being attacked by Slavic pirates, and weakened by encounters with Turkish fleets.

Art and pleasure
Decline was gradual but inevitable. As the volume of trade shrank, the Venetians began to exploit the attractions of their fabulous city. Palaces continued to rise along the Grand Canal and throughout the city. To visitors, Venice seemed even more gorgeous and magnificent. Opera was born here as music and theater flourished. The great composer Monteverdi was choir-master of St Mark's church for 30 years in the early 1600s. A century later Vivaldi presided for nearly 40 years over one of the orphanages for girls, which were famous as schools of singing and instrumental playing. Venetian art, too, enjoyed a second flowering in the brilliant views of the city painted by Canaletto and Guardi.

The end of the Republic
For all this, however, real wealth had stagnated, and 18th century Venice was principally a notorious center of pleasure. By the time Napoleon swept through Europe, the

Below: This photograph, taken in 1890, shows tourists in the Piazza San Marco. Such people were the first modern tourists, but tourism was not new to Venice. Even during the Middle Ages, crusaders and pilgrims on their way to the Holy Land of Jerusalem were encouraged to stay in Venice for a few weeks to enjoy themselves.

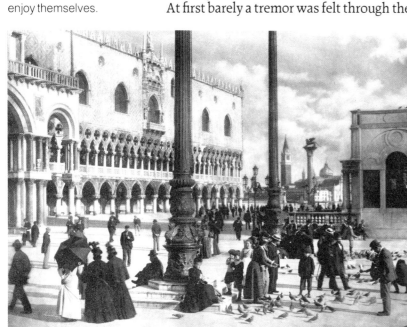

once-great Republic could offer only token resistance. The last Doge abdicated on May 12, 1797. The city was then plundered of its art treasures, much as Constantinople had been plundered by Venetians nearly 600 years before (although almost all Venice's treasures were later returned). Now Venice was contemptuously handed over to the Austrians, who occupied the city for the next 70 years.

Modern Venice
And so the history of modern Venice began. In 1848 a causeway was built linking the Venetians to the mainland by rail, and in 1866 Venice was absorbed into the new kingdom of Italy. In the 1930's Mussolini added a road, constructed beside the railway, and a new canal was cut through to the Grand Canal.

Throughout this period ordinary Venetians quietly adapted their lives to a city shorn of its wealth, but otherwise intact. Only a few were involved in the development of the Lido into a fashionable summer resort; and fewer would have been aware of the steady trickle of artists and writers discovering the poetic charms of this faded glory of another age.

Above: The four horses of St. Mark's church were brought to Venice after the conquest of Constantinople in 1204. They became a symbol of Venetian power, so the conquering Napoleon took them to Paris, where they stayed for 13 years. They were also removed from St. Mark's, for safety, during both World Wars. Here, one of them is being lifted back into position in 1945, after World War II had ended.

Left: *The Stonemason's Yard* by Canaletto. This painting gives a glimpse of ordinary Venetian life in the early 18th century. The big church (minus its *campanile*, which collapsed in 1744) is now part of the Accademia, the main art gallery. Some of the other buildings are also still there today.

Tourist Venice

Below: The area around the Doge's Palace and St. Mark's church is packed with a crush of tourists throughout the summer. Guided parties gather to tour St. Mark's and the Palace, or to catch a boat to the Lido, Murano or Burano. Nearby, *vaporetti* drop off thousands of day-trippers for their few hours in Venice.

There is a danger, of course, in such numbers. These ever-increasing crowds may one day ruin the very city they have come to see.

Venice has attracted curious and pleasure-seeking visitors for centuries. In the 18th century, young noblemen included its entertainments as the highlight of their European "Grand Tour;" later, writers were drawn by the melancholy decay of this extraordinary lagoon city, and art-lovers by its rich store of paintings and architecture.

The tourist invasions

Today almost everyone, it seems, has either been to Venice or will one day go there. Many people still come on pilgrimages, as art-lovers and would-be writers, to spend a week or two exploring and discovering. Such people come again and again, in some cases to stay. But to these few thousands have been added the masses mobilized by the modern tourist industry. For these millions of tourists from all over the world Venice is a brief but unmissable stop on their own grand tour; a city designed both for luxury and for simple pleasure.

So every year, without fail, this city of 90,000 inhabitants receives over one and a half million tourists. They come to stand in the great Piazza San Marco; to be photographed in front of St Mark's church feeding the pigeons or basking in the Italian sunshine; to take a guided tour of the gigantic rooms and halls of the Doge's Palace; to chug down the Grand Canal in a stopping-all-stations *vaporetto*; or to watch others do the same from the Rialto Bridge. They come to buy souvenirs of Venetian glass, even perhaps to take a ride in a gondola, to sit in a vine-sheltered restaurant by a canal, wander the mazy streets at night, or listen to the café orchestras in the Piazza. In fact, they come just to be in Venice.

Right: Tourists buying souvenirs of Murano glass. Glass furnaces were established on the Rialto islands early in their history – the main ingredient, sand, was plentiful. The industry moved to the island of Murano in 1291 because of the risk of fire. Venetian glass, rich in color and remarkably light, and Venetian mirrors became highly prized throughout Europe.

Today, however, most of the products of the revived factories on Murano are colorful souvenirs, made specially for the tourist market.

Simple pleasures

The basic pleasures of Venice are simple, though many visitors never leave the beaten track and sample the simplest of all – the quiet of Venice, with its lulling noise of waters and reassuring sound of people's footsteps and voices, and the eerie quiet in many unfrequented little squares and still canals. For all visitors, however, the charm of a city without cars is probably its most enduring appeal. Just for once, it is possible to enjoy the everyday smells of food and cooking – fish, bread, pizza and pastries – all mingled with a background tang of salt water.

The ordinary inhabitants of any great city take their local sights and wonders for granted as they go about their daily business. So do Venetians, but they have always had a special pride in their city. Interested visitors are often helped to find a hidden masterpiece or ancient crypt in an out-of-the-way church; or the same friendly local will strike up a conversation – about Venice.

Tourist wealth

Resourceful and practical as ever, the Venetians have adapted beautifully to the annual invasion. They gratefully accept this new booty – after all, the tourist trade has brought great wealth to Venice since World War II – and are finely tuned to the rhythms of the tourist year in their hotels, pizza bars and souvenir shops. Such money-making is a fine old Venetian tradition: the city has always exploited its attractions. Even now, however, it is not only canals, palaces and churches that make up the real Venice – but the Venetian people themselves.

Venetians' Venice

Beyond the Piazza, the Rialto, the railway station and the parking lot – and the crowded routes between them – Venetians have Venice more or less to themselves. Large areas of Cannaregio and Castello (just about the whole northern half of the city) are seldom penetrated by outsiders. This is a Venice of small stores and cafés, workshops, boat-sheds, quiet canals, secluded courtyards, winding alleyways, simple houses and grand *palazzi*, and churches big and small. In some residential quarters there are few stores at all, such as at the back of the station near the lagoon, at the other end of the city behind the Arsenal, or in the Dorsoduro district between the Piazzale Roma and the Giudecca Canal. And wherever there are boats tethered singly along a canal, or in greater numbers (for instance by the wide, sleepy San Pietro Canal where two wooden bridges arch over to the oldest part of Venice, the island of San Pietro) – these places, too, make up the Venice of Venetians.

San Marco and the Rialto

The teeming district of San Marco is the center not only of tourist Venice, but also of Venetian Venice. The vast, elegant Piazza is a

Below: Age groups, as much as family groups, provide the background to Venetian life. These men probably meet each other most days – in the morning, or evening, or both – to while away time together. Some will be close friends, and all will be close neighbors. They are likely to have known one another throughout their working lives, and now watch the world go by from the comfortable background of their local café.

Above: A back canal in what might be called ordinary Venice. But there is no city quite like Venice, and to outsiders very little seems ordinary Clothes hung out to dry have always been a part of the Venetian scene – look at Carpaccio's 15th century painting on page 9.

Venetian meeting place. The narrow streets leading from it are lined with fashionable stores, not just for tourists and the well-to-do residents of this district, but for the whole city. There are also banks, offices and movies tucked in among the steep-sided lanes.

The Rialto district remains the business center it has always been. Tourists may think they are in the "real" Venice because of the famous Bridge, St Mark's, the Doge's Palace – or because of the thousands of other tourists. They are, however, in a real Venice they may well fail to notice: the little pastry shops and food stores, and the offices and schools, where Venetians are living their daily lives. Many of these familiar aspects of city life are almost invisible to someone from a modern city, because Venice has changed so little outwardly to adapt to them. No such problem arises when it comes to the railway station, and the bus terminal and parking decks at the Piazzale Roma, yet these, too, are essential parts of Venetian Venice.

A local people
The very nature of this strange medieval city built on water, only two and a half miles by one in extent and densely packed within a maze of streets and canals, protects it from outsiders. Equally, the six *sestieri* (districts) are protected from each other – there even used to be differences of speech between

them. And the parishes within the *sestieri* themselves have developed distinct identities, each complete in itself, with the main church and its square as center of community life. So there is a strong sense of locality: people from high-rise Mestre across the causeway are called *campagnoli*, country folk, and even those on the Giudecca Island are referred to by some as *"Guideccini,"* not true Venetians. There is also a distinctive Venetian dialect, blurred and softly spoken, in which the usually precise Italian double "l" in a word like Castello is slurred over, *casa* becomes *ca'*, *angelo* is pronounced *anzolo*, and the church of the Saints Giovanni and Paolo is shortened to San Zanipolo.

The Venetian world
Like most Italians, Venetians now belong very much to the modern world and enjoy all its benefits – washing machines, televisions, computers, trips abroad, and so on. They remain, however, proud to be Venetians first. More remarkable than the survival of Venice itself is this survival, in a world of rapid change and amidst hordes of tourists, of a people as local as might be found in an isolated mountain village. The Venetians may now have cars parked at the Piazzale Roma for shopping expeditions to the mainland and ski trips, but they still find Venice (and its lagoon) a complete world.

Left: These women and children form a typical family group. In other parts of the *campo* people will be sitting at open-air cafés or restaurants, standing talking, sitting reading, playing, shopping at market stalls or simply passing through.

How does it work?

Venice works because it has to work. Connected to the world by road, air and sea, it operates by water today, as it has always done. All the normal services of a modern city have been adapted to canals, narrow crooked streets, bridges (about 400 of them) and old buildings.

Essential services

Electricity is carried on pylons from the mainland, and goes underground at the Giudecca. For centuries, water was collected in cisterns beneath the stone well-heads in every square and courtyard. Later it was brought by boat, and sold by water carriers. Today the water boats have gone, the well-heads are sealed up, and the water is piped from the mainland and stored in reservoirs on an island near the Lido.

Venice serves the world as a center for both culture and pleasure, but the lagoon city produces little beyond its unique pleasures. Even the big modern docks near the railway station, with their warehouses, silos and refrigeration plant, are dwarfed by Mestre's port of Marghera just across the causeway. Indeed, most necessities, from pasta flour to video recorders, come from elsewhere. The passage of goods is almost entirely one way.

Across the causeway come vans, trucks, tankers (with gasoline for boats and oil for heating) and trains. Once at the Piazzale Roma – the terminal for all motor vehicles – the complicated process begins of breaking down the loads into smaller and smaller portions, to fit barges, boats and hand trucks. Fresh produce goes down the Grand Canal to the markets by the Rialto Bridge; other goods go to small warehouses and stores all over the city. Bulkier merchandise also comes by sea. But everything, whether bathroom basins, building bricks, or theatrical sets for the city's famous opera house, must reach its destination by water.

A working logic

Police, fire, ambulance and funeral services are all waterborne. Rubbish, which the tides used to be thought sufficient to sluice away, is now swelled with tins, polythene, plastic and glass. So, reversing the process of goods coming in, today's rubbish goes from neatly-tied bags in back alleyways to carts, and into dumpsters on rubbish barges. Some of the vegetable rubbish is sifted out and taken to fertilize the nearby market-garden islands. The hard rubbish goes to build up new islands, like the parking lot at the back of the Piazzale Roma: typical Venetian ingenuity and thrift.

Everything is worked out to the last detail – Venice would be impossible otherwise. There is usually a Venetian way of doing things, as for instance the postal numbering system. The city is divided into six districts, and within each all the houses are numbered in strict order from No 1: the Venetian answer to the unruly jumble of a city made up of nearly 30,000 such addresses. Venice may seem to be a romantic city, but it has always survived by severe, practical logic.

Above: A fireboat becomes a speed-boat when there is an emergency. The fire station is just off the Grand Canal, on the Rio Nuovo, where the fireboats wait under open arches, rocking on the swells of passing water traffic. The firemen's pumps are used as much for flooded buildings as for fires.

Right: All the bridges of Venice are stepped at the sides, and hump-backed to let traffic pass underneath. So the carts that carry small goods through the streets have to be built for the job. The small wheels at the front keep the load steady between steps, while the big wheels at the back take the strain.

Above: One of the working barges of Venice. They carry everything, from crates of beer and soft drinks to new washing machines. Some are run as small family businesses. This one is delivering building materials.

Left: A funeral on a winter's day. This funeral barge is one of the larger, more ornate kind; ordinary motor launches, painted black, are used as well. The funerals of important or wealthy people usually go in solemn processions along the Grand Canal, before the barge ends its journey at the cemetery island of San Michele.

17

Mud, clay and quicksand

The first wattle huts were raised on a few rudimentary stilts, or sat on a row of logs which had been swept down to the lagoon in floodtime. But brick – and then stone – structures needed stronger foundations, so whole pine logs laboriously brought from the nearest forests were driven deep into the mud, the river silt of millions of years. The brick and stone themselves were, as often as not, salvaged from settlements on the mainland.

Later, the lagoon dwellers learned of the qualities of the stone from the Istrian peninsula just across the Adriatic. Istria soon became one of the most valuable parts of the Venetian Empire. The window and door surrounds of Venetian buildings are still renewed in this pale, marble-like stone today, impervious to salty water and salty air; and for 800 years it has provided the foundation stone at water level.

A forest of wooden piles

The wooden piles themselves – oak or pine, also from Istria – were driven down to solid ground; a layer of clay as much as 100 feet down, called the *caranto*. By the 17th century when the church of Santa Maria della Salute was built, with its great dome and mighty stone scrolls, we are told that 1,156,672 piles were sunk. The church is still supported by this underground forest, preserved in mud.

Beneath the *caranto* lies a layer of quicksand, which supports the ten foot thick clay by adjusting its upward thrust as the resilient clay takes weight from above. Thus the "stones of Venice" ride on a raft of clay. In some areas this raft (which can be punctured) is harder than others, for example in the Dorsoduro, or hardback, district. Generally, however, it has compressed over the centuries, although not evenly: the skyline shows no true vertical lines (many bell-towers have collapsed), and the 800 year-old mosaic floor of St. Mark's undulates like a magic carpet.

Towers aside, the medieval buildings survive. The foundations cannot last indefinitely, but the traditional materials and techniques have stood the test of time. The Venetians never felt the need to change the plan or style of the classic Venetian house. They had developed something that worked for Venice, so there was no point in pulling it down and wasting valuable building materials.

A sunken city

Today the grander structures, like St. Mark's church, are maintained and repaired by a combination of old-fashioned iron clamps, delicate manual skills, and new technology such as x-ray analysis. Reinforced concrete is sometimes used in water-logged basements, as the "ground" floor of a house on a canal (which means all the finest buildings) is too damp to live in. For Venice has sunk: the sheer weight of the city has gradually compressed

Right: A typical 15th century Venetian *palazzo*. The supporting piles were oak when the distance down to the *caranto* was not great, and pine when they had to be much longer. Sometimes the lines of piles only supported the main, outer walls of the building.

After the piles had been driven down to the clay they were leveled off, and the tops packed round with clay. Then, on a "raft" of wooden planks, the brick foundations were built.

Inside the building wood, rather than brick or stone, was used for walls, to reduce the weight of the building. The beautiful open arches also helped to lighten the load, and provided light for the grand main hall.

Left and below: The great *campanile*, or bell-tower, of St. Mark's collapsed on July 14, 1902. It had been the city's light-house and watch-tower for over a thousand years. No one was hurt. The Venetians decided to rebuild it exactly, but with improved foundations.

Much of the beauty of Venice is the result of practical considerations. A *palazzo* like this was designed to house not only a rich merchant and his family, but also the merchant's business.

The main front door, on the canal, led to the warehouse, with storerooms on both sides and a small mezzanine floor above for offices.

The family lived on the large first floor, with a grand reception hall in the middle behind the balcony, and smaller side rooms.

The narrow top floor was for servants, the warehouse clerks, and extra family relatives.

the clay, so that the water level is now much higher than when most of Venice was built.

This century the water has "risen" as much (over eight inches) as in the previous ten centuries. The rate accelerated alarmingly during the past 30 years as enormous quantities of water, extracted by mainland industries, drained the natural reservoirs in the *caranto*, causing it to contract and harden more quickly.

The water extraction has now been stopped, but there are indications that the level of the Adriatic itself may be rising. And in the city there is continuous damage to the crucial water line, as the waves of thousands of motor boats eat into the stonework.

Little of this is apparent in the everyday life of Venetians, except in the immediate problems of heating damp buildings in the winter, and plumbing in a city with no proper sewerage system. These faded and peeling buildings are too well built to fall down, yet they belong to a vanished age.

Right: Pile driving. The piles were first soaked in water, and have lasted well over the centuries. The method shown here is still used today for driving single mooring piles into canals.

Left: Restoring a damaged pier at the side of a canal. A temporary wall is sunk into the bed of the canal, and the enclosed water is drained out. Then the mud and silt covering the damaged pier, wall or foundation is removed. Great care is needed when working near the base of a building, for the protective clay and mud must not be scraped away from the wooden piles. If that happens, the foundations may disintegrate.

Canals and boats

In the first place, the canals were just irregular channels between low, muddy islands. Water and land often merged at high tide. But as the islands were built up and their shores were walled around, the canals took permanent shape. They remain to this day, however, basically channels between islands, most no more than a yard or so deep. Even the river-like Grand Canal has an average depth of less than nine feet, and some canals have been filled in – any street called a *rio terrà* was once a canal. They function both as waterways and the principal drainage system of the city, and each canal is itself dammed up, drained and cleaned out every 20 years or so.

Lagoon traffic

The open lagoon, half mud at low tide, is scored with deep channels for oil tankers, warships, luxury cruise liners and cargo ships, and the car ferries which shuttle between the car terminal and the Lido. They have to be dredged continually and are marked by lines of *bricole* – triangular clusters of massive, seaweed-hung piles chained together and topped by warning lights. Traditional fishing barges (*bragozzi*) use the channels as they head out to sea, but the fishermen of the lagoon in their smaller boats know the many unmarked channels intimately.

City transportation

Passenger transportation around the city (the *Circolare*, or circular, route) and up and down the Grand Canal is provided by *vaporetti*, or water buses. These famous diesel boats are the basis of the public transportation system. Strictly speaking, only the stopping-all-stations one, which takes nearly forty minutes for its zig-zag journey down the Grand Canal from the railway station to San Marco, is a *vaporetto*; the express boats on the same route are *motoscafi*. Double-decker versions (*motonavi*) take passengers from the south side of the city to the Lido, and from the north side to Murano and the other islands.

Within the canal network of the city itself there are many different smaller boats: large workaday barges carrying necessities throughout the city; little *sandoli*, traditional all-purpose carriers rowed with two crossed

sandolo

bragozzo

oars by one person standing; red fire-service boats, ornate black and gold funeral barges, ambulance boats, police boats, water taxis, tiny private boats with outboard motors (moored at regulated places in the city and used mainly on the lagoon); and of course gondolas, symbol of the city.

Traffic control

Just as cars have increased elsewhere, so have boats in modern Venice – with the attendant noise of sirens, horns and churning motors. Yet with speed restrictions and the simple traffic rule, gondolas to the left and motor boats to the right, there are few accidents. There is even a solitary traffic light – on the Rio Nuovo – and rush hours, as Venetians go to and from work, morning, midday, midafternoon and evening. For them the *vaporetto* is no more for sight-seeing than a subway train. But although they always pay less than visitors, Venetians long for the off-season when they can have the chugging boats to themselves.

Above: *A traghetto* is a gondola, adapted to ferry passengers from one side of the Grand Canal to the other. There are six *traghetto* crossing routes which have been used for centuries, for there are only three bridges across the Grand Canal.

Right: One of the deep water channels of the lagoon runs down the Giudecca Canal, and past the Doge's Palace. Here an Italian warship dwarfs the many everyday boats – *motonavi*, gondolas, a rubbish barge, motor launches and, at the bottom, two delivery barges – one refrigerated.

vaporetto

bissona
(ceremonial Regatta boat)

Gondolas

One of the loveliest scenes of Venice is a
gondola gliding under a bridge at night, the
sweet sound of the accordion and singer heard
long after the tiny light of the gondola has
disappeared around the next corner. If there is
no music, then the only sound is the hollow
knock of the gondolier's long oar in the
oarlock, a faint splash and swish, and the
gondolier's melancholy warning cry as he
turns the corner: a simple *A-oi!* impossible
to imitate.

Gondola construction

The origins of this graceful, shiny black craft
are shrouded in mystery. Nobody even knows
exactly what the metal prow signifies – is it a
scimitar, a bishop's crook, a coat of arms? The
present simple ornamentation was fixed by
law in 1562, and the basic shape has not
altered much since then. Like all the boats of
the lagoon it is flat-bottomed, light but strong,
and easy to maneuver.

   The most precious single item in the
gondola is the *forcola*, the wooden oarlock
shaped something like a javelin thrower's
bent arm – and no gondolier ever leaves it
unguarded. The most skillful surviving
forcola-maker carves this strange, abstract
Venetian form from a single piece of walnut,

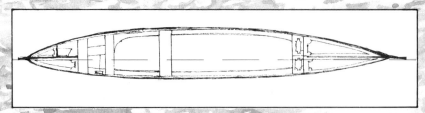

Above: From above, the
shape of a gondola is
clearly "off-center." The
last change to the shape
was made in the 19th
century.

Left: Gondoliers near
the Doge's Palace. Most
of the gondola ranks are
on the Grand Canal, for
all the customers are
tourists. Like taxi drivers
in other cities,
gondoliers never seem
to try hard to find
customers – but they
seldom wait for long. In
the meantime they chat,
dressed here in their fine
weather uniform.

Right: The gondola yard at San Trovaso. In the days when the gondola was the normal means of water transportation in Venice there were many yards and over 40,000 gondolas. Today no one has a private gondola, and there are only about 200 gondolas in use.

This yard, and one other nearby, are the only ones still building and repairing gondolas. Yet the skills, the tools and the techniques (280 pieces of seven different kinds of wood go into the making of a gondola) have not changed.

Left: Gondolas have looked very much like this one for more than 200 years. The color of the fringed cushions (black, red or blue) and the gondolier's strip of carpet may vary, but everything else is regulated by law. The boat itself is licensed, and the license paper is often wedged under the flower holder, as here.

A gondola can seat up to six people, with five seats and a simple bench opposite. The ideal passenger number is two, for a quiet, leisurely half-hour or hour through the canals. The heavier passenger will be asked to sit on the right, to help balance the gondolier on the left.

On summer nights, flotillas of up to eight gondolas, each packed with tourists, are a common sight. An accordion player, and a singer, are often included in the price of such excursions. On the Grand Canal, before going into single file for the narrow side canals, the gondoliers can wheel the whole flotilla around without breaking the line.

and now takes orders from art-collectors as well as gondoliers.

As to the boat itself, many different kinds of wood go into its making. The dimensions are precisely laid down, 35 feet long by 4.5 feet wide, but lopsided to counteract the weight of the gondolier as he stands high out of the water on the left-hand side of the narrowing stern.

A family business
The skills of the gondolier combine delicacy and strength, like the boat itself. There is never a bump or scrape, and on the Grand Canal there are many seemingly miraculous escapes from launches and *vaporetti*. As the gondola is now used only for pleasure, gondoliers cannot work in the winter (or on rainy days) and must charge very high prices. Anyone can become a gondolier, but because there are so few new gondolas built each year the profession usually stays in families. In fact, nothing is more characteristic of modern Venice than the gondolier fraternity – completely dependent on the tourist trade, but at the same time a society to themselves.

Daily life

Above: The 8:00 a.m. rush hour, as office and shop workers take the water-bus down the Grand Canal to the Rialto and San Marco business districts.

Left: A misty Venetian dawn, as the city begins to wake. A loaded cart trundles over a bridge, and a few early workers start their day.

The Italian day begins early and finishes late, with a break of about two hours in the afternoon. In Venice, as elsewhere, there are cafés and pastry shops where people stop in first thing in the morning (or later in the day), usually to stand at the counter for a cup of coffee or a light pastry. If it is their local café there will be many cheerful greetings and handshakes. As in any traditional town or village, early morning shopping is done for fresh bread, and for the ingredients of the midday family meal.

Left: Florian's café in the Piazza San Marco is a famous meeting place, used by wealthy Venetians as well as by tourists.

Right: After the midday break, workers return to shops and offices, which open again for business from about 3 p.m. Here, meanwhile, two of the thousands of stray cats in Venice are fed a few scraps left over from the lunchtime meal.

Above: Dusk in the Campo Santa Maria Formosa, with a Communist Party fair adding to the usual social life of a Venetian evening.

Right: A corner of the Campo San Polo in the late afternoon. Older children will be kicking soccer balls about in the open space of the *campo*.

Above: Mid-morning shopping, with fresh fruit and vegetables, washing powder, mops – and local chat – all available.

Space and privacy

The patterns of daily life generally take place in more intimate spaces than in other Italian cities. The human voice dominates the urban noise of Venice, as it must have done in every medieval town. Laughter and shouts echo between the paved alleys and high buildings. Wherever possible, life is lived in the open: sitting at a window watching the world go by and talking to friends down in the street; on the wooden roof terraces; and of course in the *campo* below.

The Venetians, like most Italians, delight in talk and conversation. They also seem to dress with extra care and color, perhaps because they are constantly "on show" – they don't even have the privacy of a car ride.

Right: School is over at 1:00 p.m. for these children. Their school is probably no more than a few streets and bridges away from their homes. After lunch, the main family meal of the day, their afternoon is free. They may do homework, help with household chores, or play.

Right: Not everyone lunches at home. These Venetians are eating in a local restaurant, and of course waiters and kitchen staff are working in hundreds of places like this, all over the city.

Below: After lunch many Venetians rest indoors, and shops close. In the Campo Santa Margherita the owner of a morning fish stall hoses down the deserted paving.

Growing up in Venice

Venetian toddlers are more closely watched than others, since water is never far away. From the very beginning, however, children are taken in carriages and strollers to the local *campo* in the early evening, when the whole neighborhood gathers to chat and play. Soon, at the age of three, they enter the first of the many kinds of school in Venice. For the next two years they attend the parish preschool from 9:30 to 4:30 each day, taken home at lunchtime by parents or friends.

School and play

When normal schooling begins, at primary level, the hours are 8:00 until 1:00, and after going home for the family meal – the main one of the day – Venetian boys and girls have the afternoon free. Later in school life there will be homework to be done. But at this carefree stage they play in the courtyard outside the door, or in a street or alleyway around the corner, always in sight or earshot of mothers, aunts or grannies at windows above.

Space is very restricted, yet the parish is a world in itself. The church is a familiar, friendly place, often with a supervised playground in the convent or school next door. Above all, the wide open *campo* is the place for small children to ride bikes (although

Right: Most of the preschools and nurseries in Venice are run by the Roman Catholic Church, and staffed by nuns. Here, a nun is taking a group of preschool children on a short excursion – perhaps to the local church for singing practice.

Below: In Italian towns, the whole neighborhood gathers in the early evening to stroll, talk, and meet friends and relatives. In Venice this takes place in the local *campo*. Here in the Campo San Polo, mothers, aunts, grandmothers and a few teenage girls look after the smallest children, who become part of the local community from their earliest days.

Right: Two children have capsized their kayak in the Cannaregio canal. Now they are being helped to drag the boat, full of water, from the canal. Playing about in boats is a natural part of almost every Venetian childhood.

strictly speaking these are banned in Venice), and for others to rollerskate or kick a soccer ball around.

At middle school and above, the wider world of the lagoon beckons. Summer afternoons are spent swimming at the Lido, taking an old boat out to the shallows to fish, gather mussels or fool about, or practicing in a traditional Venetian boat for a rowing regatta. Small parties of older boys and girls will take a motor boat into the lagoon on a summer evening, perhaps with a radio, simply to go for a ride and get some air.

Holidays
The schools, buildings like any others, are dotted everywhere through the city. In the winter they keep everyone warm and the gymnasium provides a place for exercise – or there will be a trip to the big new indoor sports palace near the Arsenal (or to the soccer stadium itself). Venetians live life in the open as much as possible, but foggy and freezing afternoons are spent inside, watching television or playing computer games, and on Sunday going to the movies.

Summer vacations are a problem, as most families are involved in some way with the tourist trade. The usual alternative is two weeks in the mountains in winter, even if children have to get permission to miss some school time. Many hotel and restaurant owners take their families as far away as Africa to seek the sun.

A crowded home
Venetian children are aware of the tourists from their earliest days: these people you cannot understand, often in large groups led by a loud, gesturing figure with a raised umbrella; never the same faces for more than a few days, crowding the city and taking up all the seats on the *vaporetti*. But Venetian children learn to take all these visitors for granted, and to live in a world of their own. Even if one day they have to leave Venice for a job or a new house, they will always remain villagers from a magic city.

Left: A soccer game, held on the island of Murano. One of the teams is sponsored by a restaurant, the other by a pizzeria. After the match, most of the players and spectators will take the short boat trip back to the main island where they live.

The markets

Some market produce comes by boat, from the mainland or the sleepy market-garden islands across the lagoon. Most, however, comes into Venice across the causeway from the fertile Veneto plain between the lagoon and the mountains – roughly speaking, the mainland of the old Venetian Republic.

The wholesale markets

The markets of Venice have always been beside the Grand Canal in the middle of the city. Close to the north end of the Rialto Bridge lies the fruit and vegetable market; behind it are the butchers' shops (there are slaughterhouses near the docks) and cheese merchants. Then farther around, under colonnades, the catches of the ancient Venetian fishing industry are displayed on slabs and trays.

Boats of all sizes bring in fish from the Adriatic, called *pesce azzurro*, and from the lagoon itself. It is a rich variety, ranging from tiny squid, sardines, shellfish, crabs and scampi (the original Venetian shrimp) to giant tuna chopped into scarlet steaks. There are trout and eels, too, from the nearby rivers.

As in any old city, the early morning markets show the local people at their busiest and liveliest. When the first visitors and shoppers arrive the bulk fruit and vegetables have been loaded onto barges and boats, for shops and street stalls all over the city. As the wholesale business winds down, a large market for local shopping is set up alongside the Canal, the cheapest and best in the city. The street leading from the Bridge is lined with stalls selling glass necklaces, fruit and vegetables, leather work, cheese, flowers, hams and sausages.

Local shopping

Since they have no cars to fill up with supplies, Venetians, more than most Italians, maintain the frugal habit of buying only what is required for the next meal. Shopping need never be far away, in the local *campo* or *ruga*, and social life feeds on these many little excursions. Stalls usually sell fruit and vegetables daily, fish once or twice a week, and trinkets and simple clothes on other days. The occasional small supermarket is friendlier and less tidy than in "normal" cities.

Venice is not famous for fine cooking – perhaps because it has never produced its own food. Neighborhood restaurants are modest, and full of Venetian family life.

Left: Most fruit and vegetable stalls are set up on dry land, but this one floats on a side-canal beside a small *campo*. The owner, like all Venetian produce sellers, buys from the wholesale market each morning, and loads up his boat in the Grand Canal. The journey to his regular mooring spot beside the Campo San Barnaba takes about quarter of an hour – and he then sells direct from his boat. An awning shades his produce from direct sunlight.

Left: The early morning scene at the wholesale market. You can see part of the Rialto Bridge in the background, and the main post office building across the Grand Canal. Launches have already delivered the first postal collection from the Railway Station and the Piazzale Roma. Meanwhile, the everyday market routine of unloading and loading barges and small boats with fruit and vegetables is in full swing.

Below: The main fish market, with morning shopping in progress. Many Venetians prefer to buy directly from the Rialto market, where they can select from a vast range of fresh sea foods, such as the squid on the trays in front of these women.

Lagoon life

The lagoon is essentially an unlovely place, a shallow, muddy backwater, part salt and part fresh water. Yet for over a thousand years rivers have been dammed and diverted, massive sea walls built, and channels constantly dredged in order to keep the lagoon in a delicate balance between land and sea. Without these interventions Venice would long ago have been destroyed by the tides, and the whole lagoon silted up.

The Lido, Torcello and Burano
The outer barrier of the lagoon was once simply a line of sand bars, or *lidi.* Now the upper one is a long island called the Lido. It provides the people of Venice and the other islands not only with one of the best beaches in Europe, but also a place where they can enjoy the trappings of 20th century life.

The islands and marshes on the other side of Venice, however, reveal a different aspect of the lagoon: its rich and poignant past. A boat journey to deserted Torcello represents an escape from the noise and rush of modern life. In the early history of the lagoon there was a city here, which rivaled the city on the Rialto islands for centuries. The first inhabitants of Torcello named the six surrounding islands after the gates of the Roman city from which they had fled. But the lagoon silted up, malaria

Above: The island of Burano. The simple buildings have nothing of the faded, peeling charm of those in Venice. They are always painted in bright, fresh colors trimmed with white. This fishing community lives a life quite different from the city life of the Venetians.

Left: The Lido beach. There are thousands of cabanas, several grand hotels, a casino, and sports clubs. Many Venetian families rent a cabana for a month or two during the summer, and spend much of their free time on the beach.

broke out, and now scarcely a trace remains of these once busy and prosperous lagoon towns. Only Burano survives, with its neat little canals and streets lined with brightly painted houses; a lively fishing community famous for its lace-making and with very strong local traditions.

On Torcello itself, only a few farms and restaurants now surround a small church and a vast cathedral. Yet the very size of the melancholy, half-eastern cathedral and the faded splendor of its interior, especially the huge mosaics, remind visitors of the importance of the first city in the lagoon. Torcello is far enough away for Venetians to ignore completely – perhaps this was always so. Only tourists take the hour-long journey from the north side of Venice to seek out the strange quiet of the place.

The satellite islands

On the way there and back, the boat service stops at the two satellite islands of Venice – Murano, large and untidy, its glassworks still economically important to Venice; and even closer to the city, the small cemetery island of San Michele. Here only the rich and famous have permanent graves. The bones of all other Venetians are removed after ten years: at one stage to remote Sant' Arianna, one of the original six islands of Torcello.

Many other islands dot the lagoon – between Venice and the Lido the four Islands of Sorrow, housing hospitals and mental institutions; near Burano a monastery island supposedly visited by Francis of Assisi; and here and there small islands with crumbling villas or hunting lodges, now favorite Venetian picnic spots. There are also marshes, wild birds and lonely fishermen. In winter, fog can make it seem like a haunted place, but on bright Sunday mornings it becomes the playground of Venice, with motor boats buzzing everywhere.

Above: Looking towards the island of Burano from the *campanile* on Torcello. Immediately below is reclaimed marsh land, now used for growing vegetables, and a channel laid with tidal fishing traps. A stretch of shallow lagoon, neither mud nor water, is followed by permanent reedy marshes, cut through with navigation channels deep enough for boats.

This marginal land has the important function of soaking up high tides. Further schemes to reclaim large areas for industrial use have therefore been resisted.

Seasons and weather

It is not eternal summer and high season in Venice. Eventually the days close in, dark and cold. Few tourists are left, gondolas are dismantled and stacked away; there are no window boxes or bird-cages to be seen. Most hotels have closed and their staffs departed, leaving the Venetians (and a few enthusiastic visitors) to themselves.

The northern winter
If they are lucky, there will be many days of crisp sunshine right up to Christmas, the snow-covered Alps glistening on the horizon. But sooner or later cold, rain and fog set in for weeks. Venice is very definitely a northern city. Occasionally some of the smaller canals freeze over.

In the days of glory, merchant families would leave the city in the stifling heat of summer, for their marble villas on the mainland. Today this is the money-making time, nor is there much business to keep the city and its people in vigorous activity through the winter months, when the world ignores Venice. While the owners of *palazzi*, many of

Above: It often rains in Venice, in any season – but the dogs of Venice don't have umbrellas! This one, at least, has freed itself from the muzzle they are supposed to wear by law.

Left: A misty day by the Doge's Palace. Venice has a ghostly feeling when mist and fog descend, a regular happening in the winter months. Bells and sirens sound mournfully through the blinding fog of the lagoon, and sometimes all water traffic ceases – even the passenger services on the Grand Canal.

them foreigners, may close shutters and leave the city for warmer places, most people of course stay on. For days on end the *bora*, a cold wind from the northeast, blows down the Grand Canal.

But then there is the glow of Christmas. The whole Venetian community is reunited as everyone comes home from the mainland and abroad. In Venice the celebrations begin on Christmas Eve, with present-giving and a sumptuous seafood dinner, followed by the usual feast the next day. For once, the visitor may feel like an intruder. A few weeks later the damp and gloom are challenged again by the masked revels of the Carnival.

Spring and summer

Finally, there is spring. Venetians believe it arrives on May 15 – a beautiful month in Venice as the year begins with bright, fresh weather. Life in the *campo* and on the lagoon revives, and the business of welcoming the world can get underway again.

Summer has its moods too, for Venice, like a ship at sea, is prey to fierce, sudden storms. And there is the *scirocco*, a strong, persistent wind from the southeast which tries everybody's patience. Later in the year, in combination with high tides, it causes the frequent floods which threaten the very existence of Venice.

Above: The domes of St. Mark's after snow. Although snowfalls do occur they are not very common, and seldom get very deep or stick for very long.

Festivals and celebrations

Venice was made for show, and Venetians have never needed much excuse for festivals or celebrations. Some have been magnificent affairs. In the days of the Republic, the State Barge sailed out to the mouth of the lagoon with a brilliantly decorated armada of smaller boats. There, in an elaborate ceremony, the Doge cast a gold ring into the sea, renewing the symbolic "marriage" of Venice with the Adriatic. This was not only a solemn religious event. The Venetians were also displaying the pride and wealth of their city, for their own enjoyment and to impress others.

A bridge of boats

Much the same is true today. However, one at least of the surviving festivals is truly a Venetian family affair. On the third Sunday in July a bridge of boats is constructed across the wide Giudecca Canal to the Church of the Redeemer, built to commemorate the end of a plague in 1576, which had claimed thousands

Above and right: The Vogalonga, which began in 1975, is an annual rowing marathon, not a race. Thousands of rowers in over a thousand boats of all kinds row a 20 mi figure-eight course out to Burano and back.

The Vogalonga is a Venetian family festival, and it has revived traditional Venetian rowing among girls and boys, men and women, the old and the young. Here (right) the Cannaregio Canal is lined with the cheering families, friends and neighbors of the returning rowers. In best Venetian fashion all the crews, large or small, are wearing smart matching uniforms. Some boats are rowed by members of one family (as above), while others represent sporting clubs, hotels and banks.

of lives. During the day people walk to the church across the bridge, and in the evening everyone brings their boats, filling the wide "basin" of San Marco. A special High Mass service in the church is followed by one of the most spectacular fireworks displays of the Venetian year, and night-long feasting and parties on the boats.

The Regatta and the Carnival

The Venetians' love of pageantry and their flair in putting on a marvelous show live on, especially in the Regatta and the Carnival.

The Regatta is held on the first Sunday in sunny September, with the Grand Canal free of traffic and lined with thousands of spectators. An "historical" procession of boats and stately barges, with costumed crews, introduces a series of traditional rowing races up the Canal. In a very different way the recently revived Carnival enlivens two weeks in Febuary.

Both festivals are, of course, very good for business. So are the modern festivals of art and literature, held every two years in elegant pavilions in the Public Gardens, and the annual film festival on the Lido. More than ever, Venice needs its festivals.

Above: The recently revived Carnival is a time for everyone to put on weird masks and elaborate theatrical costumes. Visitors from all over the world come to join Venetians in music, dancing and crazy antics all over the city. Of course, the modern Carnival is only a shadow of the original, year-long entertainments of the 18th century Carnivals. But the Venetian tradition of dressing up in gorgeous finery needs very little encouragement, and each February the city is transformed. The 20th century seems to have been banished when extravagantly dressed people like these throng the streets.

Living in a museum

Venezia non è un monumento, ma città vivà – "Venice is not a monument, but a living city." So begins a recent article in the main Venetian newspaper. The trouble is that both things are true – Venice *is* a monument and it is also a living city. The most famous and most splendid city in Europe from the 13th to the 18th centuries has survived virtually complete, a unique monument to the past. Consequently, what would normally have been replaced because of sheer age, or altered to meet modern needs, is to be preserved and treasured at all costs. This means not simply the main buildings, but all of Venice.

International aid

Since the disastrous floods of November 1966 made people aware that Venice was in peril – from industrial pollution as well as from the sea – many private international committees have been formed. They have raised large amounts of money and rescued many precious buildings and objects. The Italian Government and the Commune of Venice itself have not been slow to follow. But funds are limited, and have been devoted in the first place to the urgent restoration of churches, works of art and grand *palazzi*. the Commune and the Government also have the enormous responsibility of saving Venice from sinking into the sea. So in all these programs, from the restoration of 15th century stained glass windows in the church of San Zanipolo to colossal engineering schemes to control the flooding, the immediate needs of Venetians have usually taken second place.

Restoration and repair

Thousands of buildings whose interiors are never seen by tourists or art-lovers desperately need major repairs. Above all they need damp-proofing, a process taken for granted in all modern dwellings and of utmost priority in Venice. Many Venetians, therefore, feel trapped and frustrated, even angry. Venice must be preserved in its present form, so Venetians may not alter the appearance of their houses; yet at the same time they feel excluded from the sums being spent on everything but the all-important insides of their homes.

Below: Everyday tools – ladder, bricks and mortar – are used here in a familiar way. But because this is Venice, the workmen must stand in a boat to do their job!

This picture shows the condition of most ordinary buildings in Venice. The cement is peeling off because of the salty air, revealing the warm red of Venetian bricks. Part of the chimney has crumbled, and is being restored to its traditional shape. Clearly, too, the ground floor is not lived in.

Right: Of all the museums in Venice the most important is the city itself – every street, stretch of canal or *campo* is like another room in the gallery. Almost everything is worth studying – even this rather shabby row of houses. In fact, this 18th century building is listed in a book about Venetian architecture. And like all Venetian buildings, it is protected from alteration by strict regulations. Permission is even needed to alter the shape of a window.

Can the ancient city adapt, and yet keep its identity? It is not a simple matter, of course. Necessary new houses, for instance, would spoil this wonderful museum of a city; so would industries other than tourism. And the modern revival of Venice owes everything to the tourist trade, which would disappear if Venice were to change. Occasionally, then, fierce arguments arise among Venetians about conservation, tourism, and Venice as a living city. There has even been a proposal to modernize Venice completely, fill in all the canals, build new parking lots, and turn the Grand Canal into a highway.

The demands of the 20th century
The world claims Venice for its own, but has been forced to recognize that time, water and the modern world have caught up with Venice both as a place to live and as a museum. Without its people Venice would be only a museum; brought fully into the 20th century it would no longer be Venice. One without the other would be meaningless, for Venice is both monument and living city.

Left: Restoration work on the richly carved gateway to the Doge's Palace was carried out by Venice in Peril, a British organization. The work took three years to complete. Here, a vacuum hose and a delicate high speed drill are used to remove centuries of encrusted dirt from a statue of St. Mark. The cracking and flaking of the stone from exposure to salty air and industrial fumes are examined by x-rays, and treated with chemicals.

Because of the enormous amount of restoration work to be done on mosaics, paintings, statues and buildings, a new local industry has been created.

Mestre – industrial Venice

Every year more Venetians leave Venice and move to Mestre, the modern high-rise city across the causeway. While the population of the lagoon city declines, Mestre, like most other towns and cities in Italy, is expanding. The same geographical reasons that enabled Venice to prosper in the past have produced a huge oil port and industrial city; only now it is not silks and spices that enter Europe by the lagoon, but oil. From the medieval prosperity of Venice arose a city of unrivaled splendor which, even faded and crumbling, still enchants people. But today's petro-chemical millions have produced an ugly urban-industrial complex. It is the Venice visitors do not want to see.

The problems of money
Mestre and its port, Marghera, can provide year-round employment at good wages. In Venice, by contrast, most work is seasonal and only modestly paid. In fact even similar jobs are better paid elsewhere, since Venice, so dependent on popular, cut-price tourism, is by no means a wealthy city. Moreover it does not qualify for a financial subsidy from the Italian government as a tourist city – Rome, Florence, even Milan do, but the population of Venice is not high enough! If it were only a matter of jobs, though, Venetians would simply commute to Mestre every day, catching the bus at the Piazzale Roma as many now do. The main reason for the exodus from Venice is housing.

The housing crisis
Venetians no longer want to move in with their parents when they marry, as in the old days. They expect a home of their own. Because of the effects of a recent Rent Act, however, there are practically no houses or apartments to be rented. And buying is out of the question: only the wealthiest Venetians or rich outsiders can afford it, certainly not young couples just married. If they did manage to buy a house or apartment, they would have to spend as much again restoring it against damp and rot. So even those who still work in Venice have no choice but to move to Mestre, where a house is half the price and needs no modernizing.

If they work in Mestre, of course, they enjoy not only higher wages but a lower cost of living – Venice is dearer because of the cost of transporting all essentials. But Venetians leave Venice with the greatest reluctance. Most cherish the hope that one day they might move back. They love the city they grew up in, and do not long for modern ways for their own sake – for speed, size, glamour and noise. In fact, many young couples start working hard to save enough money to return to Venice, from the day they move to prosperous Mestre.

The price of survival?
Sadly, there could hardly be a greater contrast with Venice than Mestre, an urban sprawl rather than a city. It has few traditions, no real center and scarcely a trace of the natural unity that characterizes Venice through and through. It may be that Mestre, an example of some of the worst aspects of modern life, is the price that Venice must pay for its survival into the 21st century – no matter how many laws are passed or how much money is spent.

Below: Mestre begins here, at the end of the causeway which links Venice to the mainland. You can see the local railway station in the background, and blocks of high-rise apartments on the left. Mestre shares the same local government as Venice, and so its car registrations begin with VE (for *Venezia*).

Left: The port of Marghera. This huge industrial complex, which includes a petro-chemical plant, provides thousands of well paid jobs. Most of the workers whose cars are parked here live in Mestre, but some may commute daily from Venice itself.

Below: You can see the smoke from the petro-chemical plant at Marghera – just over one half mile from Venice – in the background of this picture. Industrial pollution, of both the air and the water, is one of the problems Venetian authorities have begun to solve. In the foreground is the Customs House, with the church of Santa Maria della Salute behind it.

Can Venice survive?

Below: The Piazza San Marco under water. The ground in front of St. Mark's always floods first in Venice, because it is the lowest point in the city. Over the centuries the level of paving in the Piazza has been raised, and it now slopes down to the entrance of St. Mark's: once, there were steps leading up to it. The trestle walkways are always kept handy, and the owners of the cafés and shops in the Piazza are used to dealing with flood waters knee-deep – or higher. But the continual damage to the church and its treasures is not so easy to control.

Few cities anywhere have kept such close contact with their past as Venice – recognizably the same city and people today as in its day of power and glory. Yet Venice is no longer of any economic importance, a tiny tourist center against the giant economies of the USA, Japan and the oil states, and in danger of being swamped by the modern world. But the modern world itself has already saved Venice in many ways – for instance in the wealth created by mass tourism, and in the restoration of buildings and works of art by high technology. It may well offer the best hope for the future.

Dealing with the problems

So far the signs are encouraging. Industries on the mainland no longer extract water from the clay bed, and the discharge of smoke and fumes harmful to Venetian stonework has been reduced. The biggest danger of all, flooding, was recognized by a Special Law

passed by the Italian Parliament in 1973. An enormous sum of money was voted for the construction of barriers at the three entrances to the lagoon. The combination of seasonal high tides (with the *scirocco* blowing up the Adriatic), the deepening of the main channels in the lagoon for huge oil tankers, and the vital inches that the city has sunk during this century, threaten Venice with eventual destruction by water. Over a hundred times a year now an *acqua alta* (high water) floods the low-lying parts of the city – in 1984 there was one in May for the first time.

The barrier scheme

What used to be a curiosity is now part of normal life in Venice. Almost certainly engineers have now found a solution. After many years and many false hopes (and more than one international competition) a final decision was reached in October, 1984. The chosen scheme will put fixed sea walls and moveable "gates" across the entrances to the lagoon. Yet the arguments still rage. The scheme will take at least 10 years to complete,

Left: An infra-red satellite photograph of Venice and its lagoon. The three entrances to the lagoon are clearly visible, and so is the straight line of the causeway which links Venice to the mainland. You can also pick out the Guidecca Island, Murano – and, in the northern part of the lagoon, large areas of marsh.

The fragile line of sandbars separates the lagoon from the Adriatic Sea. The thinner sandbar (the lower of the two) has a massive sea wall along most of its length.

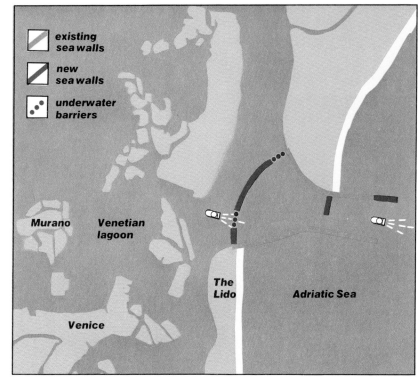

existing sea walls

new sea walls

underwater barriers

Murano

Venetian lagoon

Venice

The Lido

Adriatic Sea

and no one can be sure of its eventual effect on the lagoon. Will it upset the delicate balance between salt water and fresh water, dry land and open lagoon?

A surviving hope

Time is running out. Meanwhile, as we have seen, the life-blood of Venice, its people, is ebbing away – a problem no less serious. It is hard to believe that these people, so proud of their city, as tough as its old buildings and as resilient as the clay they ride on, will allow the city to die as a living community; any more than the rest of the world is prepared to see the buildings rot and disintegrate.

Economic reasons may condemn Venice to a natural death in the foreseeable future. But many people now believe that economic reasons are not always the most important ones. They believe that Venice should be protected and preserved because it can teach us much about art, civilization, and what humans might become in the future. What is certain is that, once destroyed, the city and its way of life can never be recreated.

Above: This diagram of the Lido entrance to the lagoon shows how a new system of barriers will keep the Adriatic's flood waters from reaching Venice. The lagoon must stay open for normal tide waters and ships, but it must also be able to close completely in an emergency. So a curved sea wall will be built inside the lagoon entrance, with two openings wide enough for the biggest oil tankers. The openings can be blocked by raising a series of underwater barriers, constructed on the sea bed. The other two lagoon entrances, to the south of this one, will be treated in a similar way.

Below: How the underwater barriers will operate. Each section of the barrier consists of a row of four giant tubes, full of water. This diagram shows one section from the side. When it is not needed, the barrier tucks neatly into the sea bed, and does not interfere with the deep water which ships need. When it has to be raised, air is pumped in to replace the water, and the free end of the tubes then rises to the surface. The complete line of tubes will then form a solid but flexible barrier across the gate in the sea wall, and keep flood waters from entering the lagoon.

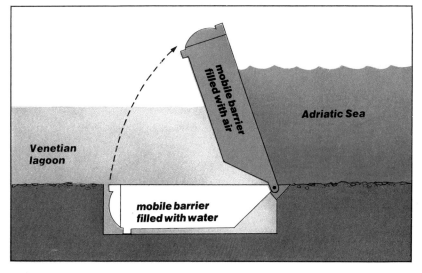

Venetian lagoon

mobile barrier filled with air

Adriatic Sea

mobile barrier filled with water

Legend

- Main canals
- Main streets and squares
- Built-up areas
- 7th century settlement areas
- District divisions

1 The docks are used by cruise liners and industrial shipping.

2 The Piazzale Roma is the terminal for all road vehicles.

3 The Railway station was built in 1848 and modernized in the 1950's.

4 The San Trovaso *squero* is one of two remaining gondola yards (see page 23).

5 The Accademia is the main art gallery. Part of the building is in the painting on page 11.

6 The markets must have been here since the earliest days, for the Rialto is the old commercial center of the city.

7 The Rialto Bridge was built in 1591 (you can see the earlier wooden one in the painting on page 9).

8 Santa Maria della Salute is a grand 17th century church.

The causeway

CANNAREGIO

SANTA CROCE

SAN POLO

Grand Canal

SAN MARCO

DORSODURO

Guidecca Canal

Guidecca Island

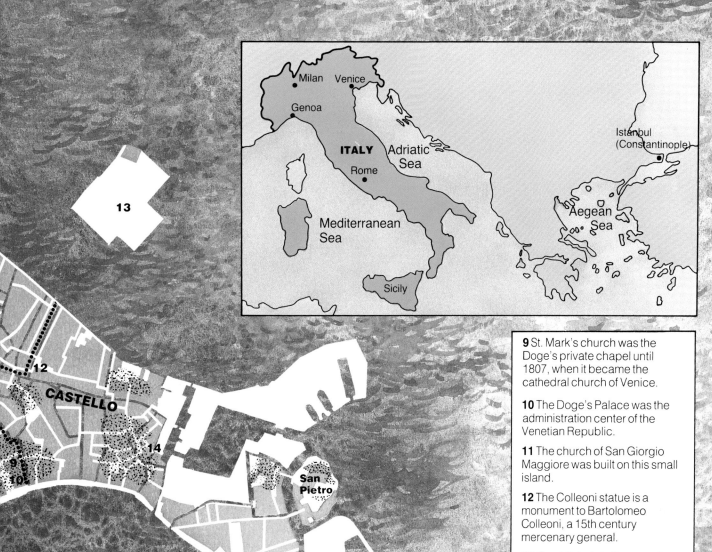

ITALY

Milan · Venice · Genoa · Adriatic Sea · Rome · Istanbul (Constantinople) · Aegean Sea · Mediterranean Sea · Sicily

13

CASTELLO

12

14

9
10

11

San Pietro

15

16

9 St. Mark's church was the Doge's private chapel until 1807, when it became the cathedral church of Venice.

10 The Doge's Palace was the administration center of the Venetian Republic.

11 The church of San Giorgio Maggiore was built on this small island.

12 The Colleoni statue is a monument to Bartolomeo Colleoni, a 15th century mercenary general.

13. San Michele is the cemetery island (see page 17).

14 The Arsenal gateway leads to the old shipbuilding yard

15 The Public Gardens were planned and laid out in 1809.

16 The Soccer Stadium is used by *Calcio Venezia*, the Venice team.

12

14

16

The language

Italian, like many other languages, has two groups of nouns – masculine ones, and feminine ones. Masculine nouns usually end with an **o** (like *lido*, the word for a sand bar). Feminine nouns usually end with an **a** (like *acqua*, the word for water). When there is more than one thing, the masculine ending is usually **i** (so sand bars are *lidi*) and the feminine ending is usually **e** (so waters are *acque*). Adjectives have to have the same ending as their nouns, and so a high sandbar is *lido alto*, but high water is *acqua alta*.

Venetian Italian, however, has its own sounds and spellings. You can see (above) the word *sotoportego* in the photograph of a street sign, but in "correct" Italian it would be *sottoportico*. Even *sestiere*, a Venetian word, has been spelled differently. Venetians also sometimes spell *croce* (cross) as *crose*, *olio* (oil) as *ogio*, and *angelo* (angel) as *anzolo* – there are many other examples.

Venetian Paintings

Many art museums have paintings by Venetian artists from past centuries. Visiting a museum to look at some of these paintings for yourself might be an enjoyable way for you to spend a Saturday, Sunday, or even a holiday. Your local librarian will be able to help you locate a nearby museum with a collection of paintings by Venetian artists.

A glossary of Venetian words

acqua alta high water, a flood.
bissona ceremonial boat.
bora seasonal cold wind from the north east.
bragozzo fishing boat with sails.
bricole three or more wooden piles chained together. Lines of *bricole* mark out channels in the lagoon.
calle street.
campanile bell-tower.
campo a square or open space, generally near (and named after) a church. *Campiello* is a small *campo*.
caranto the layer of clay beneath the mud of Venice.
casa house, in Venetian shortened to *ca'*.
fondamenta street by a canal.
forcola oarlock on a gondola.
lido sand bar. There was a line of *lidi* protecting the lagoon from the open sea. They are built up now, and one of them has become the Lido itself.
motonavo two- or three-decker *motoscafo*.
motoscafo water bus that does the express service on the Grand Canal.
palazzo large city house built by wealthy merchants or bankers.

pesce azzurro blue fish – that is, fish from the Adriatic Sea.
piazza open space in a town. In Venice there is only one, the Piazza San Marco in front of St. Mark's. The Piazzetta (little *piazza*) is the extension of it by the Doge's Palace.
ponte bridge.
rio canal. A *rio terrà* is a filled-in canal.
rivo alto high bank – from which the Rialto gets its name.
ruga street lined with shops.
San short for *Santo*, a (male) saint.
sandolo small row-boat.
scirocco seasonal strong wind from the south.
sestiere district. Venice is divided into six *sestieri*.
sottoportegho, or **sottoportego** street running under a building.
squero gondola building yard.
terra firma dry land – the mainland.
traghetto a gondola adapted to ferry people across the Grand Canal.
vaporetto water bus, originally steam-driven but now diesel-powered, which stops at all stations up and down the Grand Canal.

Books about Venice

Venice
by Herve Bordas
(Kordansha International USA, 1975.)
Islands and Lagoons of Venice
by Peter Lauritzen
(The Vendome Press, 1980)
Venice for Pleasure
by J.G. Links
(Farrar, Straus & Giroux, 1979)
Venice
by Fulvio Roiter
(Viking Press, 1979)
Venice: Its History, Art,
Industries and Modern Life
by Charles Yriate
(Richard West, 1978)
Venice: City, Republic, Empire
by Alvise Zorzi
(Abbeville Press, 1983)

Index

Numbers in heavy type refer to picture captions, or to the pictures themselves.

1 2 3 4 5 6 7 8 9 10—WOR—93 92 91 90 89 88 87 86